Weather Eye Open

NEW CALIFORNIA POETRY

EDITED BY	Robert Hass
	Calvin Bedient
	Brenda Hillman
	Forrest Gander

Weather Eye Open

POEMS

SARAH GRIDLEY

University of California Press
Berkeley Los Angeles London

University of California Press
Berkeley and Los Angeles, California

University of California Press, Ltd.
London, England

Library of Congress Cataloging-in-Publication Data

Gridley, Sarah, 1968–

Weather eye open : poems / Sarah Gridley.

    p.   cm. — (New California poetry ; 13)

Includes bibliographical references.

ISBN 0-520-24289-0 (alk. paper) —
ISBN 0-520-24293-9 (pbk. : alk. paper)

    I. Title. II. Series.

PS3607.R525W43   2005

811'.6—dc22   2004007727

Manufactured in Canada

14 13 12 11 10 09 08 07 06 05
10 9 8 7 6 5 4 3 2 1

The paper used in this publication meets the minimum
requirements of ANSI/NISO Z39.48-1992 (R 1997)
(*Permanence of Paper*).

For Joan Merrett Gridley
Meret qui laborat

CONTENTS

ACKNOWLEDGMENTS

Many thanks to the editors who first published these poems, some in slightly different forms, in the following publications: *jubilat*, *The Beloit Poetry Journal*, *Barrow Street*, *Drunken Boat*, *Square Lake*, *Goodfoot*, *Meridian*, *Volt*, and *Journal 1913*.

Most of all I am indebted to my family, friends, and teachers.

To discover an order as of
A season, to discover summer and know it,

To discover winter and know it well, to find,
Not to impose, not to have reasoned at all,
Out of nothing to have come on major weather,

It is possible, possible, possible. It must
Be possible.

WALLACE STEVENS

Cuckoo's Report

I speak in years and coins. I speak my own name
across all contexts: deuce, deuce, deuce. If you were listening
needles kept tacit guard at the forest
beginning where snow fell in two directions,
once, by volume, once, by discernment. The first was mute,
and loved the world, the other was lost,
and loved the world. Intermission fell between them,
space for the rising, space for the stretching,
space for the yawning. A cello
curved beneath the bark, varnishing a sermon.
When the cloudwork went down and was melted
on the tongue, it was known that the work
had neither feather, nor pinion. Exposure took
quick root: the wingful idea of snow
lay down in gray waves. Breath
consented, tacked in the up & cross-drafts of winter.
Better than feckless, it could stick on a tightrope.
And did it. And did it. And did it. A weather ever
recruiting new camps: Loves me, Loves me not, Loves me,
Loves me not. So could indifference grow fond.
And sweet were the uses.

Cloak

Sits at the escritoire,
mournful for livid coffee in fine-boned cradles,
the way the snow fell there. The ink rests overlong on the page.
He is barefoot, and feels desire fading. It has not snowed here.
Children live in the windows, pressing fingers
to wet glass. Plum shadows trance over indoor luxuries.
He has stepped from the steaming bath, into the drafts.

Paint dust. A bloom collapsing. The material begins again.
Light's strange maneuvers: he has adapted himself to its swan neck,
to its brown facts. It is to be tenderly beside
its not feeling him, this country tinged with rim.

He waits for permission to bowl the warm shavings,
to paste the embers into phylum, *Roar.* He remembers
delicacies. How her ear
was infinitely exposed. The whelk, now, his dearest
source of menace. Kept on the mantel
in the room made of rugs and clocks. Aria pelagic: a black
internal billowing. Were he allowed to count, he would set up
a counting table. So to rub neglected shades
by thumb & index finger.

■

Husk, scruff, sheaves. What color did we traverse today? There is,
he has inquired, no surgeon. There is, he has demanded, one
    confessional,

but found its hollow
recent abandoned. Tufting cattails. Meadows, wharves, mines:
his worship, he finds, is no more specific.

Turf dims, catkins shudder. Snapped stalks, tarns half-locked.
It is to be partial pool, partial cage. I prefer not to—he says
to no one listening—love you
by reflection. But where is there more to drink?
Even the rock, masked in crystals,
a frozen spillage, says so.

■

Perspective shuffled into fir trees. On this day he holds out
immunity to then. Gently. It is not yet snowing.
At margin a gesture
glances him red. The motion remembered
westerly, past island marshes
bristling gold. He concentrates
on this perception, how to grade
by going in. At end of day, heaped yellow in past-noon,
in the quality when. Caution: the self-abuse
in courting *after*.

■

The houses are sharp, the steeples sharper.
Today he has lived in glass. In speeding windows, has made

a veil of breathing. Out of the scrubbed gallery
spluttering oil. Out of the rooms
historically lived-in, and sinking.

There are reeds tipped ocher
into end of day. Behind him, the sea, his changeful blue, *the color of
a fig.*
Beside him, a compass: nerving northerly, easterly.

The Vernal Landscapes

Nested high in the winds, the specksynder yelled down
what flecks he found in the mirror. Occasionally, there were
    sightings:
pods like murmurs shading waves. A firm cursive

moved the captain's log. Still, in a faceless hour, green
could confuse into leisure. Then the tell-tail ceased to point.
Then the mainsail flapped its mind.

When the ocean rolled in slopes like earth, how like shepherds
we longed to sing, wet with throats that couldn't own
how our sails were visited.

When we looked to the page, it was convex-
pearl. When we looked to the mirror,
it was green: in the shade

turning love and nausea,
in the trough that was swapping
again for again.

Capsized

Mother I am dreaming: of a yellow flower
in the shearing month. What remembers? Is readable
in the last sign light swallowed: the taker's sloping posture.

A critical mass tips what? Down here, Pluto spares no effort. It is all-
bounded country: a wind-ribbed spit, a reach on which to mourn
or count the falling riches. Mother from your summer

knit me shadow's source. He has moved door
by door indoors, drawn gloss from dark-
clicking throats. I am detained

by an all-sided glamour. Lightning, a frail scar—a flashed motif
let down in jagged script: no straight bone, no clean pocket.
By what polite retracing?

Opens the bathlit nursery, the gangly mobile revolving, the almost
    familiar parts
meaning anything they can. Mother make no bones:
    mutely they displace
what needs to speak. Unstrung the vertebrae float

from a ceiling overdone with fire. Mother, the mob is who?
Fractured are the asphodels, a general surface powder
nowhere appointable.

Wanting the Ten-Fingered Grasp of Things

At this portion of the curve
where quartz is ground, the ocean brokers
broken wares. Energy is cursive, cold and beautiful.

Mare. You have imagined here
to yield up counting. Beyond the wide
disquiet of the gulls, horizon is the love of bonfire.

In the haptic scripture, all cups are running over.
To think what blood cannot accommodate.
To feel what it can.

The Body Is Placed, but the Spirit Is Emigrant

Alone as the wheat wears the moon, who opened history
to the page marked *Evening*.

Blurred pedals. Bright spits
of lung. When the world was sprawled

on top of itself, my savior was a miniaturist.
Who learned such properties of ice, how fire writes first

under skated cursives. Blade your names
across the melt. He played

the closing off, in eel light,
when the barometer made beautiful

aspirations. Heart buried in Poland.
The shambles robed in France.

Rus in Urbe

A conscious
liar, an inasmuch reserver of the truth, perhaps
you too are a hoarder. Perhaps no higher than a worm
spinning your march of raw silk shrouds.

The clock is inflicting more points
than a cruse of solar marigolds. Rain is unveiling
your favorite inventory. Let no one blame you. Into well's
moss-lit emporium, lower your private damages.

Look softly: Neptune's methane wreath
sets no red loose. Finished seconds sculpt the hour a shell
of when it was. Let wind come up to rusk the cells, rake
    since-demolished
crowns and keels. Impalpable shepherd
you have won: less crowd

more pasture

A barometer, strictly consider'd, is, in truth, nothing else but a philosophical pair of scales, wherein (by the artful contrivance of a vacuum, and the restless endeavours of nature to restore and preserve an aequilibrium) a column of air is continually weighed against a column of quick-silver.

EDWARD SAUL
*An Historical and Philosophical Account
of the Barometer, or Weather Glass*, 1735

Genealogy

To ear, the shell recounts the ocean's holdings. To eye,
the book refigures pulse, spun-black signatures outlasting
guests of body.
    She locks it in
the top-most drawer. In sleep a bullfight
brights its gore inside her. Now a face
of unparticular appeals. Her hands assess the tin case
colony: rain-bowed in cork, the angler's
feather flies. Trout like dimming
      roses skim
the edge of keeping. What falls to her possession: a thrash
& spiral script. As trees take roughness up
to clouds at spring's arrival. Written in the vertical.
Lashed to passing features.

Sortilege

Blue makes a vast endeavor
        for a spider's verbing rungs. Cloudbulks gorge
to needle-shower. Splayed
        kingdom,

give less ground to envoy. Inscripting tides
        and water-rooting
lily: what rides upon that silt night
        squanders over face-

less bone? A plot: a whole sanctuary
        lived across the dead
sewn up in grass. What will doubtless be
        be inside the things we cannot rescue. Blind-

folded, safe from the fits
        of the body. Laid by the gypsum-dusted quince, a crescent
knife. Another sandbag
        lighter by your leave, the fleets

are threading faded
        faded air. Spring. The more the fiddleheads
uncrank their serrations. The more the stone
        sits in the meadow.

Prodigal Song

Asleep by the obsolete atlas,
now you can imagine in what hour you are tempted, how far pleases
you best has shifted. Spiral-scalped apples, a barbed
wire of cloud, a gate
uplocked at dawn. What things can you take
for welcome? A shade. A bell rushed close to the eyes
is a portraiture of noise, is a window paying gaze is between you
blood. You scarcely know what takes you in. The air
is charged with versions.

The Craft Must Be Lighter-Than-Air

Duchamp speaks in the splintered pane
your chance is not the same as mine. By the aleatory method, it is all
becoming personal.

Mouth shapes a vague siphon for silhouette.
Can a body be so fervent in petition its parts revert to whole?

What flight more wind-contingent more balmed in sun
than a hot air balloon? I would.
Lording over
the dumb town I would. Fearless of stars and seas.

Myth: it was death to see the moon bathing. Yet the moon persists
in bathing us.

The petitioner is now lending
his knees. As he reaches and retreats from this midpoint, I call him
potentially seen. I give his name

a clean page of its own.

What Adjective

Hybrid of sun and moon, of verb and noun, the cup stays twilight's
divergent bodies. As lacquer is the warm lake eyes float through.
As lacquer is the insect shell eyes crack against.

Oiled water rocks repeatedly into stillness. A mirror above this
    table longs
to picture what scent. Instead: white silks shrugged off, some figure
naked in a winter month.

Do you count the walls blood raps against? The orchid
is not one stroke brown. The orange on the sill, a lost word
defacing snow.

The Eve Of

Red first touched
or earth first dammed
the ocean

brain? Radical
pavilion, your broken spurs
& lacquered flesh

You Have Given Me Such a Delicious Dish

Theorems shook off the stars. Other planets had other moons.
Around your clean-won honey dropped
a fortune in billable hours.

■

Regard the rose, skeletal, a bafflement of buttons
so little no hands
might fasten or unfasten them.

■

Your wilderness & wilderness. My office
wall. Spine without anatomy. Nile running where. I promised my eyes
to a vein. In truth we call this

knowing.
The mouth is a sluice. Is a deadly
place. Is streaming.

■

Not to be stone, but to be its loving limit. You were the sculptor
tipping the pitcher
to see how water makes intimate with stone.

You were the painter re-virgining whores
in serious chiaroscuro. Deluging inlay, outlay. . . . Not to be light,
but to be its loving

■

Heavy bells are being moved. It is the seventh day. Nothing scatters
but birds. We have said to ourselves

and said to ourselves. Dull face: take off that mask
of waiting room.

The dome far off. The dome unworshiped in. There was
no vault
I traced as far as this. Beautiful

vanishing point. How two-
dimensional & wrong the rooms
before your tangents' ecstasy zero.

Phaedrus
We are still on the seashore?

Socrates
Necessarily. The frontier between Neptune and Earth, ever disputed
by those rival divinities, is the scene of the most dismal and most
incessant commerce. That which the sea rejects, that which the land
cannot retain, the enigmatic bits of drift . . . all things, in short, that
fortune delivers over to the fury of the shore, and to the fruitless liti-
gation between wave and beach, are there carried to and fro; raised,
lowered, seized, lost, seized again according to the hour and day; sad
witnesses to the indifference of the fates, ignoble treasures, play-
things of an interchange as perpetual as it is stationary . . .

Phaedrus
And it was there that you made your find?

Socrates
Yes, there.

PAUL VALÉRY

Nocturne

All calm: glassy crests not breaking. *Smoke rises vertically*.

Into the tilting lookout
midnight throws its shining briars. Salt crystals the deck. You are tired

of dead reckoning and other
                           primitive enchantments.

At night you dreamwalk

                        through wildwood, where trees speak
in unrushed conclave. Owls crowd the hold
with eyes. Daily the sky

                        blues over these points. Sheets

stretched, masts go
almost horizontal, speed lends fleeting   sense to water.

You say what hurts
                    is being loved too well.
                        You know that paradise
            is so

against the will. But some nights you can taste the anchor's working

free of its coral bed—can swear
the word for this

                        is *music*.

Weather Eye Open

Besides the toss and drag of shells are you shown no proof
as to time lost here?

Same stamp

                        on every morning. Tattered glass
at rub on sunblind margin. No islands roofs or goat-skinned
rocks.

My stars

          but you are travel-rank!

Cracked with offering. Your hands bear
what? bow-spray? mast-scrape?

                            Keel, stinging under silver weight,

      what boat unloads your night? Why do the waves
keep you in their shattered cloak? Eyes each upon you

        creaking *pilot, pilot, pilot?*

You Are Looking for Wings on a Wolf

in lone   you swore flock

in gaunt   you wed span

in cave   you worked nest

in track   you drank cloud

in blood   you spilt air

in pelt   you dreamt down

Likeness Is the Mother of Love

The hero swims for two days. The sea appears
a hammered surface. Then an island, squid-solid, inked out, then
fish-boned, glowing in scratches. The double bears
will be shining down, dune grass loomed with their starry breathing.
Riverweeds blur and sharpen. Something will pound for him
remotely. In his mouth,
the brackish water turns fresh.

The morning will be soft-cut, dense-hued. Laurel and rock
are strewn with dripping linen. Naturally one has been named
to come across him

                                      (*Nausicaä*).

Never too worn for glamour's curve of burning
scythe through blood the hero

                                     steps in
to appearance. At his feet her singing
halts. Just
as he looks now, like this. *Be
the strategist,* he thinks. *Be
the sensualist,* he thinks, and vomits the sea
from inside him.

Gimcrack Scenery

What gracefully digressive, what windfully mathed
what sailed in full-blown division.

What stoked inside the makeshift walls: blunt gold
cold silver, what hectic clockwork half

in love with never. What craved the clicking, tipping,
trundling complication. What loved the latch,

the link, the piston and spool, the oiled teeth
and gears. What drove the water

mechanical. In tackle enshrined
its fading pulse: violet in vespered dissolve,

obverted, evanescent—a harp of sand
in barest sheen of glistening taupe

a gray smoke soldered to salt-rinsed puce
a whiteness born in diminishing blue.

The wheels, the screws, the levers, the scales:
to what end, what fed every means.

The Minors

Evening posing in the glamour getup of field lights, into dry valley

    ash echoes over mown grass, over painted

diamond, hypnagogic. By this green distinction done

    & undone all

inhale, all murmur & applause plowed deep

    down & numerous

in the air. At the plate below

    the heavens' sickle,

heart weaves to unravel its red

    bolts in patience. The boys are setting out

and coming home:

    Ulysses & Ulysses & Ulysses

Jurisdiction

you and rusted waste
places throughout your scope

you conspicuous base
ending rungs into breathing

clients you in roses'
scrape at ocean window

sand fumes bedded into milk-spray
painted into space you

commencing in the dye vats you
faithul lover to the non-

descript infurling you you sign
and erase from

Thy eyes look to me mild. Out of maize & air
your body's made, and moves. I summon, see,
from the centuries it.

JOHN BERRYMAN

Instructions for the Little Painter

Open your paint box:
dandruff devil's shoestring semen iron filings.

Never put your paintbrushes in your mouth
as many of the colors when swallowed

are poisonous. Begin at the top of the picture making
the sky first. There he appears under

the heading, Jacinth Thug.
He is sure as a soldier in a red uniform.

Keep your brush moist enough. Not so much
that it will puddle on his horse. Nothing lasts long

that isn't looked after. A pinch of mind creates
your turret of sanctity. Then fire the brush in the air:

Bang!
Looser in the sheep, further up the apples

Grist

×

Have I considered the windmills long enough to say I prefer them
as spectacles to lilies? In fact
the practical lens was preceded (naturally) by Chaucer's figurative
use of spectacle—
the "lens" through which a thing is viewed. Which begs the
question: are we moved *by* windmills,
or *through* them?

×

1588:
in his work, *The Mariner's Mirrour,* an engraver, Waghenaer, charts
windmills as landmarks
on the north-east coast of England. The captain is shaving on deck.
Above his shoulders see them turning
in reflection, fields of them planted full-sail . . .

×

As of a creature half-alive, often I think of my arms
as misplaced windmills, of air as the gentlest reproof there is. *You
are in cross-purpose,*
it says, *You are in outgoing rupture, foreign with will*

and was. I like this language; often it puts me, as a reminder, into
    a smaller
and smaller body

×

Not surprisingly, R. L. Stevenson liked windmills. One can assume
    he considered them long enough to say

There are indeed few merrier spectacles than that of many windmills
bickering together in a fresh breeze over a woody country; their halting
alacrity of movement; their pleasant business, making bread all day
long with uncouth gesticulations, their air, gigantically human, as
of a creature half-alive . . .

×

Or consider the acoustic vacuum between shook foil   &
toil   be   tween
          trod   &   trod   &   trod

×

Can be cause for misunderstanding: the work done toward the end
    & the end
called indistinguishably *the work.* Opus
Magnum. In Sanskrit

look how smoothly *apas,* work, turns into *apnas,* possession. In the
   windmill the outcome
is all indoors: ground meal rising to conditions capable of
   combustion and subsequently flame-like
licking up the sails

  ×

A merry spectacle this making bread. Finished,
it begins
again. A swoop of pigment. A flourish. A quixotic
getting at. Admittedly, I have tilted
at windmills.

  ×

The cooing I lavished on its sails!
Sword point dagger point first reef—
bone-slipper   lobe-   sling
quatrefoil   lunulate   wallower
cream   milk   chalk
scissors, scissors, scissors

  ×

I was partial to words with the postfix *form:*
gemmiform, bud-like; nubiform, cloud-like. And always to *rood,*
a splintered version of?

×

See purblind Doomsters. The eyes, or some eternal happening
between the eyes. **Inter-**

est
pose
cept
fere
mission

×

Monocular despots & desperations. Of atombattle we might deduce
  that this-
ness is a syn-
aesthetic seizure. Gesture?

×

Assorted phenomenological proverbs:
The form of a fold of linen or cotton shows us the resilience or dryness of
  the fiber, the coldness
or warmth of the material . . .

In the jerk of the twig from which a bird has just flown, we read its
  flexibility or elasticity . . .

I hear the hardness and unevenness of the cobbles in the rattle of the
carriage . . .

×

-ness: forming ns. expr. a state or condition, esp. f. adjs.
ness: a promontory, a headland, a cape

×

-ous: forming adjs. having many or much, characterized by, of the
    nature of
porous
nervous

Strung-up in trees, in endings the better to feel

×

A faint, rustling congress.
Moonlight collaging underfoot. Our vessel-tree, he tells me, when
    the eye is caught
working through its own shadow image (see Purkinje,
J. E., physiologist)

×

I have long wanted a Claude lens—

×

Art Critic adds:
Form coordinates diversity, it does not pile up facts.
That is why form comes from the artist's looking for chaos.

×

edualC ne eiv aL   *La vie en claude*

×

Look how vaguely Old English embraces the spirit of opus:
efnan: carry out produce put to work exercise practice celebrate per-
form

×

Gothic cathedrals, coordinated versions of?
Windmills, dislocated versions of?

×

Throw factoids to the wind (art critic enters
again): *The Gothic man left wholeness* [Opus Magnum] *to God.*

×

A "mirrour" takes possession of?

×

operon: a unit of coordinated genetic activity in the chromosome.
Synopsis: carry out produce put to work exercise practice celebrate
   perform

×

(enter poet with prescription)

They say the cause of revolution is hunger in the interplanetary spaces.
   One has to sow wheat in the ether.

×

What is the task—as in tax—of love?

×

1530. In the Tyndale Bible: *taskmaster*

×

Who does collecting?
Who does permission?

×

pneumatic: pertaining to or operated by means of wind.
pneumatic dispatch: the conveyance of letters, parcels, etc., along
   tubes by compression

or exhaustion
of air

×

For you as yet but knocke, breathe, shine, and seeke to mend

×

The sails like thundering lilies!

×

Assorted E. V. Lucas theories:
*With blacksmiths we can be on terms of intimacy; millers are distant
    and aloof.*

Blacksmiths are at our doors; millers mean a climb . . .
*It requires influence and rare gifts of persuasion and charm to be invited
    up the steps of a mill*
into the terrifying abode of thunder and whiteness

×

Commandments 11−∞
Thou shalt step outside of the body

×

Enters the spectacle, uncertain as to which of us is moving

Impasto

December: a birthright to compose. What long wait precipitated
glow. Say it was scrape light flocking warm shadow.
Inside the clouds' migration, a host of figment
contours. Hem, impasto—in long attendance
to mineral powders, of eye to surface come
imperial magnolias, waxed glamorous into place.

Impastured oxen and sheep   *The great thing is to avoid*

     forgotten grazing
under Spanish moss—   *that infernal*

facility

            what did it cost   *of the brush*
to breathe?

Sulfurous air shrouds butterfly ponds. The plantation is rubble,
    and looted.
And the swans—

     cut smooth curvatures. Continuous mirrors
breeding soft

     urges below surface. Rises the crepe myrtle, seeded in char,
torqued limbs stripped,
     russet.   *Glory is*

       no empty word
           A passage for translation ex-
foliates,
guesswork milling in the margin. What does the smithy beat out

today? The gutters
are active enough
in dispatch.

Rained superfluously into
they cascade, unpiloted—
not thinking *I am seen through*
by soundless gargling down the pane.

And it was written within and without:

sulfurous air-shroud, the spiked
palmettos' runnels, this continuous dripping
with *egret* fed to the eyes. Plumes ascended
into seven perches versus
wet north wind.

Grisaille, the sky's smeary gloom, sunk bolts
of crêpeline. Tell me again the choices:
use short, small brushes.
Beware of thin washes of oil.
Choose a stubborn material, and conquer it
by patience.

December. A birthright to compose. Hem, impasto,
passion. The sky in the virgin's sleeves . . .

Approach in Removable Galleries

The hand drops the rag.

                              Motes rise. Sun slung in collides

with bulk. Work is stopped

                    and hung. In guarded rooms
                    given careful air. Between gold stalks

             of pendulum. Dust makes
love to surface: oil, skin, gilt, velvet. A vast sail

                            windless

              listing from the ceiling. Behindhand swung

out of blood, a threshing up of disassembled
bones. Of things

bequeathed:
            The mirror drinks and spends

bright coins.   The curtain while you

          look on it.

Saturation, a Dwelling Place

Diluted tortoise. The cat is gray as the clot
thunder punctures, the perfect drop-cloth for a shifting

list:

{shy red, fruit red, fraught red} The thought is red

in a tube. Whose top is small and inscrutable. Whose walls
are thronged as furnace?

The thought is blue

but there is

no such room, only the stairwell. Egypt, feather, Horus, homesick . . .

A little fire

is settling up. Painted,

and sun-blessed eaves, marble lions   there and there.

confections

from the host of convexity

(Praise him).

Miller's Ruth

What opens doors
Anonymously sifts grain and bone hap-
Hazardly vests
& divests
Gorgeously grooms & junks
Undecidedly. Rootless
Promiscuity—what profit
Turns, what profit
Thieves.

Sweet Outline Lost in Atmosphere

in the raven's sundown
gilravaging, a violet liable

to hand out proximity
& mood & love as if

no finite object
reserved it

entirely now is the season
to thieve when buds

are able to
I am & my own

looking comes from
the wall i.e.

demure
countermure

some boredoms divisible
by fog: Adam umber

ate? Trespass coloring
at a dumb rate sweet

outline lost in
atmo-

sphere.
Dear

Friend, I await at rue
du Bac "after"

my work your hand
through forest

seam: a wild boar
a nightingale

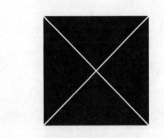

The target tells arrow, bowstring, hand and eye:
   Tat twam asi,
Which means in a sacred tongue:
   I am Thou.

ALEKSANDER WAT

Noises in Annunciation

An arrow rains in heaven, hanging its return in dotted lines.
   He comes
dashing life. With bells of sluice
and marble. Hear them? It is the coracle's freightless hymn
knocked through lost canals. His wings are black
but drizzled gold. His robes are gray but swathed in carnation.
   His cheeks flush with difficult

fire: the message is again on matter.
Into the space-binding diptych he splutters
You. Seed drops down the copper tunnel. In every chrysanthemum
I smell the shiver. I've tied some rust around my finger so as not
   to forget: dust is said
is said.

I said my alphabet is barely tried, each mark
a deep across—I said no way through this but exfoliation,
   spending perfume
in drawing rooms
whose shades are drawn halfway.

No shreds but the ones
underfoot, a sodden red and flaxen (paste I think
is willfulness, which smells of so much kindness). In ear-privacy
he marshals me: we must try now to formulate what goes—
    the clouds the book
admires between the pages, the discord in the eye
of being filled.

Locus Amenus

Two appointed, enclosed. A bordure real
and imagined. The gardened sense of privacy: lavender, burble,
    privet hedge.
Keep lungs closed against the given. A tinctured field, three wheels
    of air
in advance of rain. Drops blue, green, red. The ocean particled in
from distance. Along the slips and leaves she reads
her unwillingness to move. Conception takes
this long. The fountain: undy Argent. Her face in unfamiliar
    fractions. This is
embarrassingly beautiful. Vulned, it says, wounded.
And untouched flowers in forms too small to rescue.
Do you know the charge? Gules semy of Garbs: red field spotted
with wheatsheaves. Azure three Garbs Gold: blue field's
    wheatsheaves
in sun-soaked number. Choose where you are moved. Do you love
    the air
in forms too small to rescue? Could you bear the sound
of an empty field?

Gentle Gnomonics

The utopian speaks a utopian language.
The corner of a table and the tablecloth falling there,
Niagara.

What is the "sweetness" predicated of honey?
Each drone in queen-enslaved adagio. Each comb
a gold-cemented window.

Wild Clary

spoil   it looked after in a milder fashion

cosmos messing in the basin, wet stars moving

over marble lips

proof   one was to hold an hour like honesty in cold hands

like courtesy

to rehearse the cue in the mouth of rain

the garden   wicks sashed in smoke green to damper green

and wisdom mistaken by a half here a river split

& threaded in a train & blowing bank

golden centimeters trumpet: the end

attached   apples, then, lighting in, lightning then, starking

in see: fractious looking glass on which spinning

leaves lit

fable   a case without beginning or with

bloom turned down to burial ground:

unfed illuminants fed into corners

the adamant I was the stone

by stone the ramparts . . . I was the wing

by wing the birds . . .

holidays when one met one at the station

time   beautiful as waiting

Slipping Jurisdiction

Before the sun
was pluralized. Before the scales
packed iridescence onto land, no wings
over-spanned the wood.

No romance to a flightless planet so the skull blew up
to a sky worth scoping. *Clangs the bell.* Let the waterfalls fall.
And they fell, jointure on edge
in plain spectaculars.

The bathers crouched, dripping. Fog, the subtle aggregate,
circled their ears. Softly the tunnels
were dug. *Et in arcadia...*

Far from our lips the scribes were describing. Physical
visibility, watermark after watermark, when the rushes drink,
or drank—

$$ego$$

$$ego$$

$$ego$$

—in the scumbled weeds
a phoebe wings out of, in the downfallen glow
of a curative poison, a partial shepherding
feels nearby.

Nigh, nigh. The pond is steep
in surface. Beetles move in the bank.
Clouds spend an eternity.

Suppressed O:
Additional Turns in Outdoor Pragmatism

Invisibly raised near to the far-diffusing salt factory by sounds
liquid, unspecific. In contagious foreground, cold flowers

constellate in a straw bed. [O] domed & secret aftermath add
no reason. In flood-urged ricochet. Thus might all of us be so
   broadly

casted, so widely panicked in an unclipped dark. [O] rusted halo
   [O] swarm
of earth. Your grave and shallow symmetry. [O] deaf dog cruising
   woods. [O]

vessel: sun-glutted, unearthed by spade and moon-light leaking
   seed and summer
banquet's rivulets. In the shade the trees allow in the haze
   in the morning heat.

The poplars give poor wood, you say. But [O]
the authorless rustle.

Terrestrial

The need was coming hard to walk this far and look:
downpour stopped as glassy brown collection, reptile eyes
and jagged rudders, great herons stepping

as if green might shatter. In the drenched passage of the day, it was
a low country, plagued with rainbow. The widths the colors kept
were not locations. Not in the low country, but over it.

Sun was a foreign serum. Clouds in marsh water
mantled the marsh. The muscle heart was nearing generous:
where could we stop from walking?

This is the weather the shepherd shuns,
    And so do I.

THOMAS HARDY

There Is No Answer to What They Think

Was a claret cup—tomato, tornado, Toledo—red. Of its own
    a weather
system. Think "them." Whether impasse takes over the puddle or
    speeches the mirrorful
side-step. *Surely.*

Little bloom, incensed, suffused, why do you thirst alone?
Surely what they saw was every bit contagious. There to
    recommence or to push.
Off in the morning waves.

C: when this page slaps with possibility, that sky suffers a blue
    seizure. Observe the cleats:
how they cower into dock. And dock into harbor
and harbor into bay.

How the hills are favorably *scriptural* today!

In a scheme the desert sweet milks its throats (there there) to make
    enough.
Spring is re-debut of cups & infernalities, mostly green. Of enough
    shall we say
the conservative impulse of paradise? Jealously against the drab &
    gruff
a meaning. Full: water stowed. *Vanities.* A creature. Driven and
    derided by—
sigh, a clustered eruption of.

Say such lapses lacquers laughters were not. Work might ever
be rendered. Otherwise say *I*—say *All hours for inhabiting*
    there. Therein to limn
the forms I say the so-called *still life* that won't play

still the helixed lemon peel, the tamped clay pipe, the urn-
like shell O worldly) worldly) worldly)

life. U is a rough
and unbound C. Ever torching, ever hopping, with a *thrum*
& sliding of fingers along the frets

Codlings

In the early days
we agreed to apprenticeship. At the party
we stood apart
under fast clouds searching
for description. You
hit on *ruinous.*

Later
in the front yard
we waltzed poorly as cars
drove wondering by.

Etude

Many decimals can compile the heart.
The sun now clotting on the car's silver hood

will farm its imperial look anywhere. Blessings on the floor-
to-ceiling window

between us. In the craved anonymity
of a public space, I am drinking

water and watching. Not snow *fall*
but snow *kindle* snow *up-*

glinting, ambient as new flies, day-sentenced,
sticking wing to air.

The morning opens undictated
as skull-wires tripped

by love of motioning trees.
Any weather can induce my love.

The morning opens
in the flurry of waking.

Death and the Maiden

Prestidigitation struck him favorably: silk scarves drawn
as continuous apologies from a cane. He craved Mercatorings:
the oilskin's rolled coordinates, the peninsulas jeweled with
   feldspar . . .

He was not without interest, the storied space
between *blasphemous selfhoods.* But he poured from the vine
where the niceties stopped.

In her top drawer, inherited slips, bodiless, perfumed. *Caleche*
it was, calash, barrouche—at any rate,
an open carriage.

Once glass and water were a narrow corridor underfoot. Aquarium
to pre-ignited feathers, to yet un-lofted bodies
in the flame threading water named

carp. This was deliverance from position. This was circulation,
   the farce
and poignancy of bubble. Enchanted to make your, she begins.
If you don't mind, he defers.

Chatterton

To think kindly
on plagiarizing angels & dead batteries
though they wince at our touch we have their (if

propitiated rightly) all-divided attention. Plenum:
a dream in disproportionate occurrence. Window
stained open breeches squid blue

hair torched furious as *the day*
is coming repeats Cézanne *when a carrot freshly observed*
will set off a revolution. Perspiring weeds

where fervors ought
to cross. Love, your wings
are hectic-stale.

Wind splattering leaves to pane
to witness what? No hasp:
this air is open.

When will you
lie still? This much ghost
per garret. How

burnish?
Why garish?
In good company, in ever-

lasting draft—your white
sleeves stumbling
in the ink.

Dialogue of Comfort

A black so black in the mouth and ears and pupils
Yes

At erasure's intimate wield, all islands would from flood
Provided

A face makes a wall inhabitable
To live in, eventually, yes

Long Division

1.

Indoors, the knife escorts the apple
out of its skin, the cuttings on the counter,
a picture in oils. Outdoors is a moon,
transient red in the earth's umbra, a body
relieved from shine.

2.

Swelled to land then crushed under tires
with the sun, the shells came up
from the globe's loose province. Inside of occupation, they loved
preoccupation, in the daily boneyards, the hay
and the wool.

3.

To think of snake pits—
pits in the snake's upper jaw housing sensors, readers
of blood's crowding flowers, mere and warm
in the semi-dark, where prey was a thermal quote
at the base of trees, a heat-phrase
in the snake's head, a not-superfluous halo posed
on top of starker sight.

4.
Where they had touched
(they forgot)
the garden's great inches, on the farm where black
and orange wings were light-
weight clutter above
the rhythmic sweep of steel. Forgot the arc
of human invention, cool extension
of body,
gleaming as it meets the wheat.

5.
Look: scarcely red thermometers: how the slight oracles
speak of weather, in more pieces
than cathedrals, what keeps like math
to the sum of happening—born at the field's
rimed edge, and eras
above it, in the shrapnel chorus of the stars, in the sky's
increasing hinges—

6.
Blue pines. From the angel's
unsmudged pot: fish gall for the eyes
in the kingdom of data. Inside of occupation . . .

7.
Blue, blue. The oaks
no longer obscure it: winter stages
an all winter long. In generosities of snow,
in the sun-jilting ice
that frays by April into river. Vainer
than warpaint, bright is the stash
uplifting dark.

8.
Wind like a snuffbox stiff with life.
Trout when the trees first bud. When the soul vows
the world won't have them. What takes custody
of the eyes when the eyes swear
off? Bump
and rotation of ice.
Violet rills plowing sand.

It shall be said that gods are stone.
Shall a dropped stone drum on the ground,
Flung gravel chime?

DYLAN THOMAS

A Fine Cage Won't Feed the Bird

Winter citrus in opulent rinds.   Later might be

shut away
                              from distraction. As books might be spining
for hands to feel, your guest might be also
going hungry. And for it

                    showing red   by the fire

might set
                    to the keys. Might they give to his lightest
pressure.
                                        The notes look shaded
down with sound. Around the black-tailed darts you mean
to quench the lamps. In that trap
                    better to flood the over-
sight that holds you
                                        here.

Between Sail and Tiller

In the motionless tomb, oars were to pull on
space. When sands again assembled the fervid horizontal,
brain was to bight at merest gleam, skull, to be packed
with pounded spices.

Skin was to sleep in ocher. Through net
of faience beads, stripes were to run gold and obsidian.

Eyes were to indicate *open*.

In the vertical after, garland of garlands, the balanced
heart was to fall from use. Spine in search of tributary,
thinned gold sheets were to replicate tongue.

Industrial Magdalene

behind the Area of Expertise
the Passion spent by all things harnessed

was the Breathing of the Last Hurrah
& Gearing Up of Elemental

Vagaries. Go then
& ask the good workers

Are you grinders
or gilders?

The sun climbs up
for anything—

the coin for water
is game is rife is dam is

gone—the route for water
runs cleverly—ruins not but takes the going

tenderly. Scruples not, nor
stops there: weds, unweds, whores.

Swayamvara

Hello, Lovely.
Thank you for leaving that tone in my machine. I?
am dealing blackjack. A breeze is tampering with a chandelier.
   A crowd
has gathered, all gloved. A peacock fans on a green felt table,
   all eyes. A strange power
lights the garden. Need I say who, in the corner, coughing?

A cigar box opens.
The eyes raise. And I chose you. As if to explain flowers inlaid
in a lady's cabinet. Or peace in a dripping grotto. Or evacuation of
   the flesh
through secret, ivory keys.

Remember, Dearlungs, the body un-architected? Piled in a glass
   case, the played-out reeds?
The grass? The hoppers? The thousand stops?
Hello, Lovely.

Hello.

Jupiter

put us not
into or inside of

old lullaby tactic
the world rocking apparently

gentle now
in the snow stopping

gently (it would) the fire
fed up

in the system
under the skylights

shut with white
the cells still want

dusk suppering
the lookful sun

bending woodward
the blue

grapes drifting
black &

vertigo
the approximate thrill

in the sea
of tasting them open

Psyche Speaks of Eros

Where I opened his look in the dark, Love blessed me
Foolish. My exit began with smell of wings
like filmstrip burning.

Through exit I stole, snuffed in accordion pleats, his arrows
and his gentle ink. Let them flicker.
Thus I kept him

crumpled close, godlike with looks and unintended
aim. Of periphery, beyond the tissue maps of two hands held
against horizon, I can best say nothing. What I see

is absent capacity: mint leaves in cracked cups, oil sinking
green illumination into bread, the black goats'
miniature copper bells.

Please forgive the scattering fables. I fear *satisfaction*
is a misbegotten compound, *Love,* a texture,
not a transfer.

As ever the gods are good at recompensing—at feeding
silvers to the upturned palm.
One word for this is *rain.* But often

 a surface belies a surface. See *entrance:* a means
by which something is entered. Then *entrance:* to affect
with wonder, to carry away.

What Is Lost in the Fire Must Be Sought in the Ashes

The wood-reeve kneels at the yew, scoops snow from its roots
to cool his face and throat.

In the hall, fox-red ale surpasses cups, rivers into table grain.
The musicians alone have not been drinking. At stiff strings
they summon joy from little joy.

The harpist in his mind invokes Saint Dunstan: patron
of armorers, jewelers, lighthouse keepers.

Straightening, the wood-reeve ends his thoughts with words:
What tidings, rook, what tidings?

By commute of mirror to mirror, a small fire powers
a spacious caution on the waves.

From the solid silence of the yews, icicles tune coldly
in the flying off.

NOTES

CLOAK
I live in company with a body, my silent companion, constant and exacting.—Eugène Delacroix, *The Journal of Eugène Delacroix*. London: Phaidon Press Limited, 1995.

THE VERNAL LANDSCAPES
Title borrowed from *Moby-Dick,* chapter 113 ("The Gilder"): "Oh, grassy glades! oh ever vernal endless landscapes of the soul."

WANTING THE TEN-FINGERED GRASP OF THINGS
I am indebted to architect Louis Sullivan for the phrase "the ten-fingered grasp of things."

THE BODY IS PLACED, BUT THE SPIRIT IS EMIGRANT
Chopin, subdued by his familiar demon, was a true specimen of Nietzsche's übermensch—which is but Emerson's Oversoul shorn of her wings.—James Huneker, *Chopin: The Man and His Music*. New York: Dover Publications, 1966.

WHAT ADJECTIVE
The Chinese have one word, *ming* or *mei*. Its ideograph is the sign of the sun together with the sign of the moon. It serves as verb, noun, adjective. Thus you write literally, "the sun and the moon of the cup" for "the cup's brightness."—Ernest Fenollosa, translated by Ezra Pound, *The Chinese Written Character as a Medium for Poetry*.

YOU HAVE GIVEN ME SUCH A DELICIOUS DISH
A jealous lord killed his wife's favorite troubadour, and had the dead man's heart served up to her on a dish. The lady ate it without knowing what it was. Her lord having told her, "Sir," she said, "you have given me such a delicious dish that never shall I partake of any other." —Denis de Rougement, *Love in the Western World.*

NOCTURNE
This poem draws some of its language from the Beaufort Wind Scale, named for its inventor, Admiral Sir Francis Beaufort (1774–1857). The numbers of the scale, 0–17, represent variations in wind force, each number accompanied by a description of corresponding effects on land or sea. Beaufort 0 represents calm, wind less than 0.6214 mph, with smoke rising vertically.

GRIST
The art critic: Fairfield Porter, from *Art in Its Own Terms: Selected Criticism 1935–1975.*

E. V. Lucas, quoted in C. P. Skilton's *Windmills and Watermills.*

Poet who enters with prescription: Osip Mandelstam, from "The World & Culture."

Phenomenological proverbs: Maurice Merleau-Ponty, from *Phenomenology of Perception.*

IMPASTO

Saw the Velázquez. . . . It has swept me off my feet. This is what I've been searching for so long, this firm yet melting impasto.—Eugène Delacroix

Italicized portions of this poem are drawn from *The Journal of Eugène Delacroix*. London: Phaidon Press Limited, 1995.

SWEET OUTLINE LOST IN ATMOSPHERE

Dear Friend,

On the way to get my Ladies to bring them back here next Wednesday, I shall be passing through Paris, and would be delighted to come shake your hand on the rue du Bac, between six and seven in the evening, after your work. If you do not have that moment free, would you let me know at the rue de Rome?

If not, you will see someone from the forest, something between a wild boar and a nightingale, who is

Your

Stéphane Mallarmé

Letter to James Abbott McNeill Whistler: May 29, 1898.

EPIGRAPH TO PART SIX

Thomas Hardy, *Weathers*.

THERE IS NO ANSWER TO WHAT THEY THINK

Title borrowed from Gertrude Stein.

CHATTERTON
After Henry Wallis's painting *The Death of Chatterton* (1856).

DIALOGUE OF COMFORT
Titled after and inspired by an Alan Magee monotype.

ACKNOWLEDGMENTS OF PERMISSIONS

The epigraph to Part One is from *The Collected Poems of Wallace Stevens* by Wallace Stevens, copyright 1954 by Wallace Stevens and renewed 1982 by Holly Stevens. Used by permission of Alfred A. Knopf, a division of Random House, Inc., and by permission of Faber and Faber LTD.

The epigraph to Part Three is from *Dialogues* by Paul Valéry, Pantheon Books Series XLV 4, 1956. Used by permission of Princeton University Press.

The epigraph to Part Four is an excerpt from "Homage to Mistress Bradstreet" from *Collected Poems: 1937–1971* by John Berryman. Copyright 1989 by Kate Donahue Berryman. Reprinted by permission of Farrar, Straus and Giroux, LLC, and by permission of Faber and Faber LTD.

The epigraph to Part Five is from *With the Skin: Poems of Aleksander Wat* by Aleksander Wat, translated and edited by Czeslaw Milosz and Leonard Nathan. Reproduced with permission from Ecco Press.

The epigraph to Part Seven is an excerpt from "Shall Gods Be Said to Thump the Clouds," by Dylan Thomas, from *The Poems of Dylan Thomas,* copyright 1953 by Dylan Thomas. Used by permission of New Directions Publishing Corporation.

"To James Abbott McNeill Whistler: May 29, 1898," by Stéphane Mallarmé, from *Mallarmé,* edited by Mary Ann Caws, copyright 2001 by New Directions, copyright 2001 by Mary Ann Caws. Reprinted and used by permission of New Directions Publishing Corporation.

DESIGNER: Nola Burger
TEXT: 10.25/13.5 Filosofia
DISPLAY: Filosofia
COMPOSITOR: BookMatters, Berkeley
PRINTER AND BINDER: Friesens Corporation